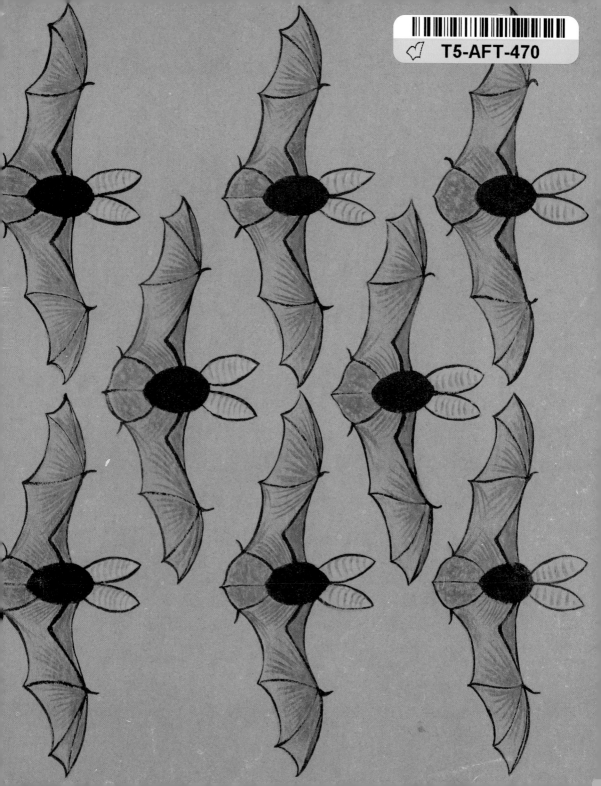

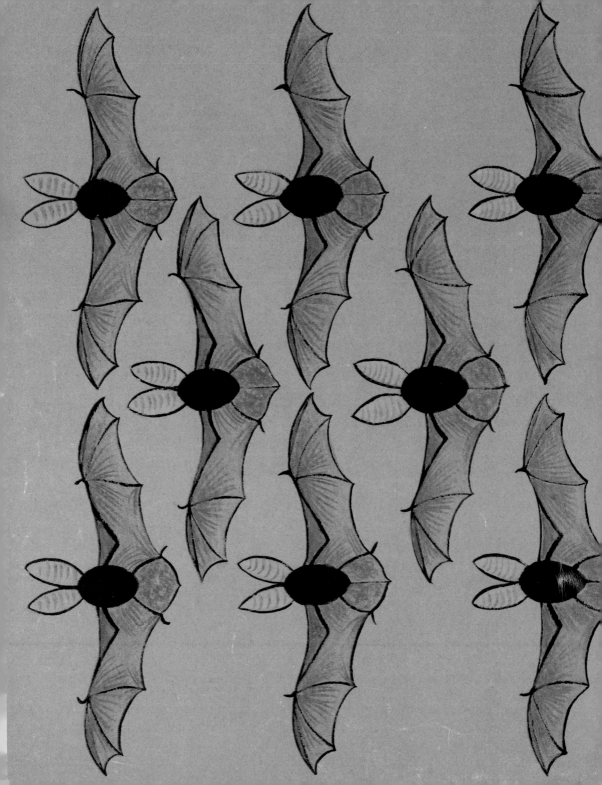

BATS

based on the Long Eared Bat

designed and written by Althea
illustrated by Barbara McGirr

Longman Group USA Inc.

Published in the United States of America by Longman Group USA Inc.
© 1985, 1988 Althea Braithwaite

Originally published in Great Britain in a slightly altered form by
Longman Group UK Limited

ISBN: 0-88462-176-6   (library bound)
ISBN: 0-88462-177-4   (paperback)

Printed in the United States of America

88 89 90 10 9 8 7 6 5 4 3 2 1

Library of Congress Cataloging-in-Publication Data

Althea.
   Bats / based on the long eared bat.

   (Life-cycle books / Althea)
   Summary: Describes the appearance, behavior, and life cycle of this bat and how
it uses its huge ears to find insects.
   1. Plecotus auritus--Juvenile literature. 2. Bats--Juvenile literature. [1. Long-
eared bat. 2. Bats] I. Althea. Long eared bat. II. McGirr, Barbara, ill. III.
Title. IV. Series: Althea. Life-cycle books.
   QL737.C595A47   1988   599.4   88-13859
   ISBN 0-88462-176-6
   ISBN 0-88462-177-4 (pbk.)

Notes for parents and teachers

Life-Cycle Books have been specially written and designed as a simple, yet informative, series of factual nature books for young children.

The illustrations are bright and clear, and children can "read" the pictures while the story is read to them.

The text has been specially set in large type to make it easy for children to follow along or even to read for themselves.

2

In the spring
the long eared bat
ends its winter rest.

Bats fly, but they are not birds.
Their wings have no feathers,
but are thin skin stretched
between the bat's long fingers
and its legs and tail.

The hooks on a bat's thumbs
and the claws on its feet help
a bat hang from branches or
catch and hold what it eats.
Soft fur covers a bat's body
but not its wings.

Bats can fly and swoop in darkness
at great speed without bumping
into one another or anything else.
They can hear how close things are
and know their size and shape by
squeaking and then listening as
the sound echos back to them.

Many bats catch flying insects
to eat. They dip low over
water to drink as they fly.

The long eared bat uses its
huge ears to find insects.
It hovers and picks caterpillars
or moths off leaves of plants.
It can eat while flying, but
will carry a moth to a
perch to chew off what it
likes and leave the rest.

In summer, groups of long eared
female bats find a warm place in
an attic or building to have their
young.

They hang downward, clinging to
the rafters with their feet.

Other kinds of bats will use one
cave year after year to raise
their families. Hundreds and
hundreds of bats share the
same cave.

When a baby is ready to be born,
the mother curves her body up
to hold on to the rafters with her
thumb claws as well as her feet.
This makes a cradle for her baby.

The baby bat is born blind.
Its mother helps it to climb up
and nestle in her fur to
suckle milk from her.

On cold days the bats all
hang close together in a huddle,
and this helps keep their
young warm.

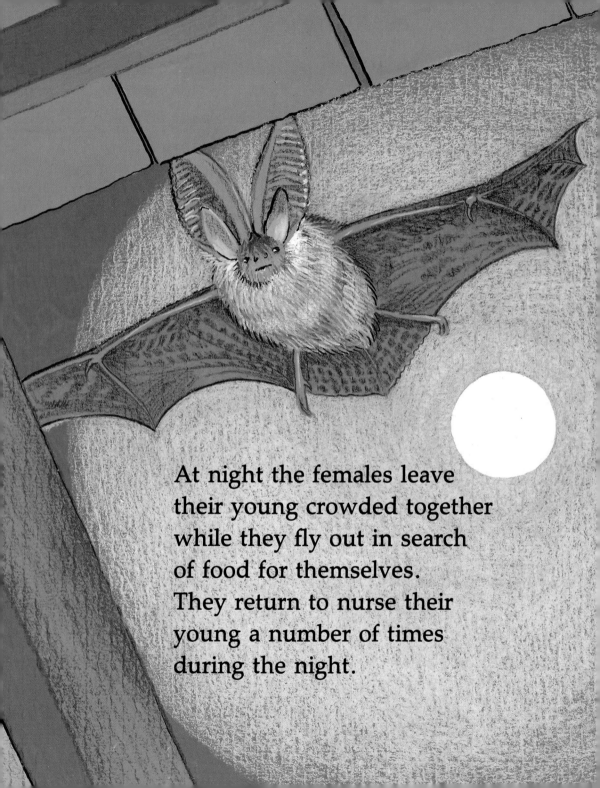

At night the females leave
their young crowded together
while they fly out in search
of food for themselves.
They return to nurse their
young a number of times
during the night.

The young will start to fly
when they are about
three weeks old.

When they can feed themselves,
they and their mothers all
go off and join the males.

Bats sleep during the day
in nooks and crannies.
They wake at sunset and
chatter together as they
clean and groom their fur.

They leave in search of food
as night comes.
They return to the same
roost each morning.

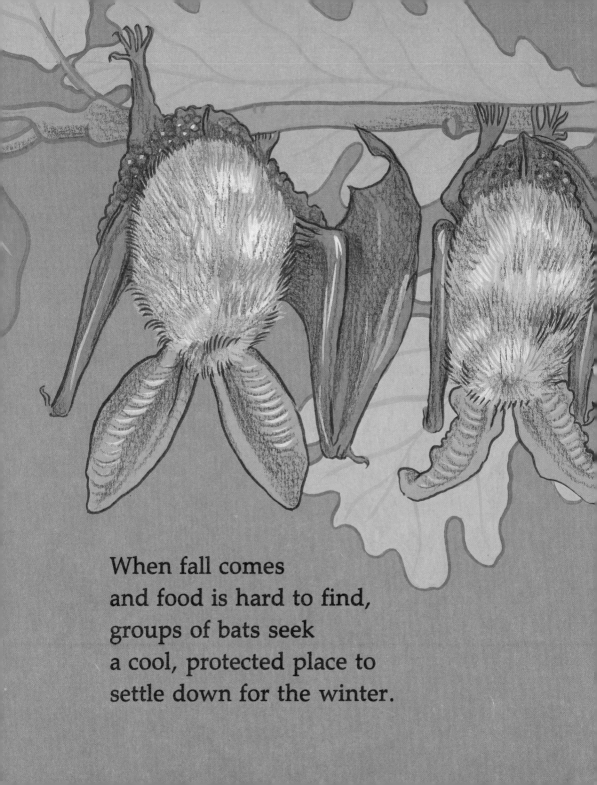

When fall comes
and food is hard to find,
groups of bats seek
a cool, protected place to
settle down for the winter.

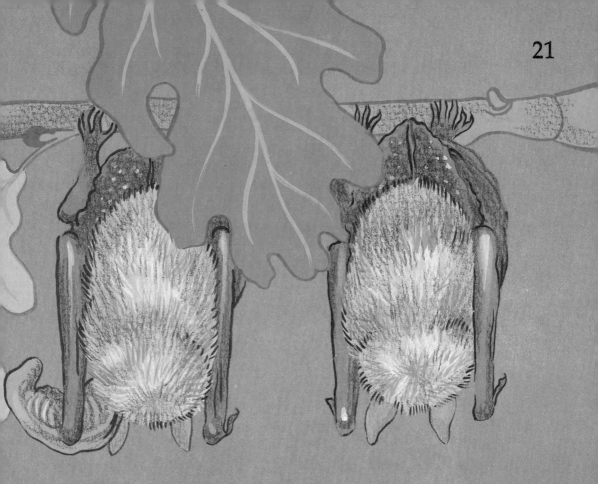

They will hang their feet
from the rafters of buildings
or in the branches of trees.
The long eared bats fold
their ears back under
their wings before settling
for their long winter rest.

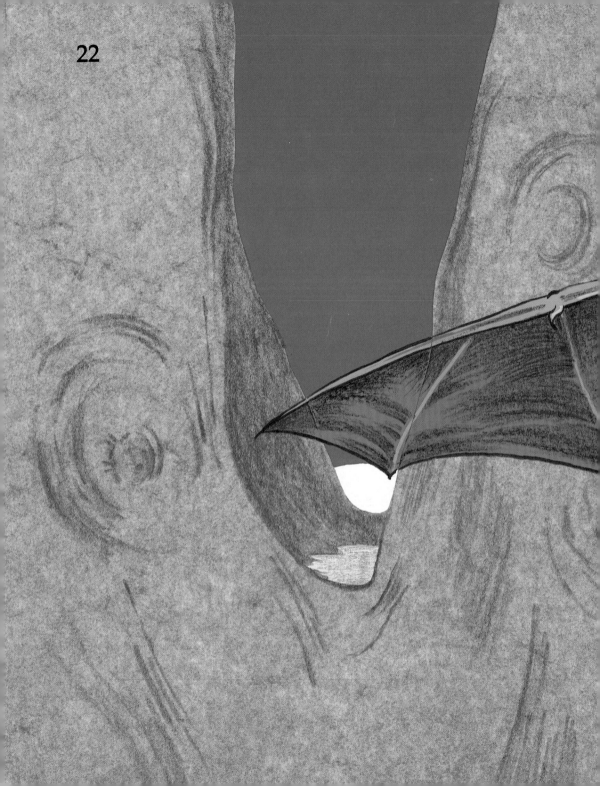

On mild winter days
bats may stir and fly out
to find water.

There is little food about
because most of the insects
are hidden away.

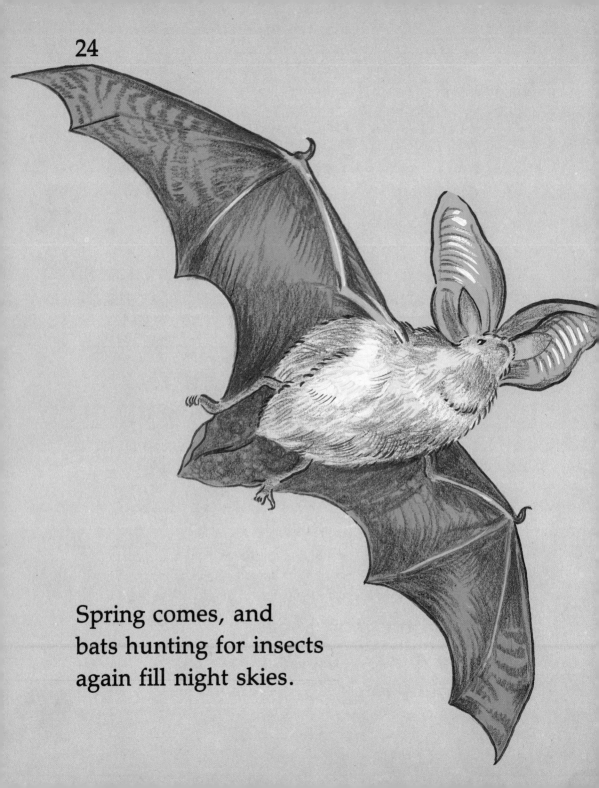

Spring comes, and
bats hunting for insects
again fill night skies.

BATS are unique among mammals because of their ability to fly. It is a popular myth that bats are blind; and while it is unwise to pick up a sick or dead bat, the fear that all bats are infected with rabies is much exaggerated. Vampire bats that attack humans exist only in fiction. Bats are in fact useful to man. Insect-eating bats help control mosquitoes and other insect pests; bats that eat nectar and fruit are essential agents in pollinating tropical trees and plants and in seed dispersal. Bat droppings found on cave floors, called guano, make excellent fertilizer.

Bats are of many kinds and they live in hot as well as in cool regions. Most are insect eaters, but some prefer fruit and nectar, and a few eat small animals. They vary greatly in appearance and size. In contrast to the long eared bats pictured here, others have small ears and large eyes. Not all bats are nocturnal, nor do all depend on sound for safe flight.

Some bats roost in places such as barns, others find shelter in trees. An undisturbed cave may house literally thousands of bats. They congregate during the day to sleep, and in northern winters to hibernate. In spring, female bats commonly gather in special caves called nurseries, where they give birth and care for their young until they are independent. Bats are surprisingly long-lived; some reach thirty years of age.

How nocturnal bats locate prey in the dark and avoid objects in their way was a puzzle until recently. They use sound reflection by sending out high-frequency calls to produce echos received by their sensitive ears.

Because bats are useful to man and frequently threatened by thoughtless destruction or man-made changes in their environment, there are now organized efforts for their conservation.

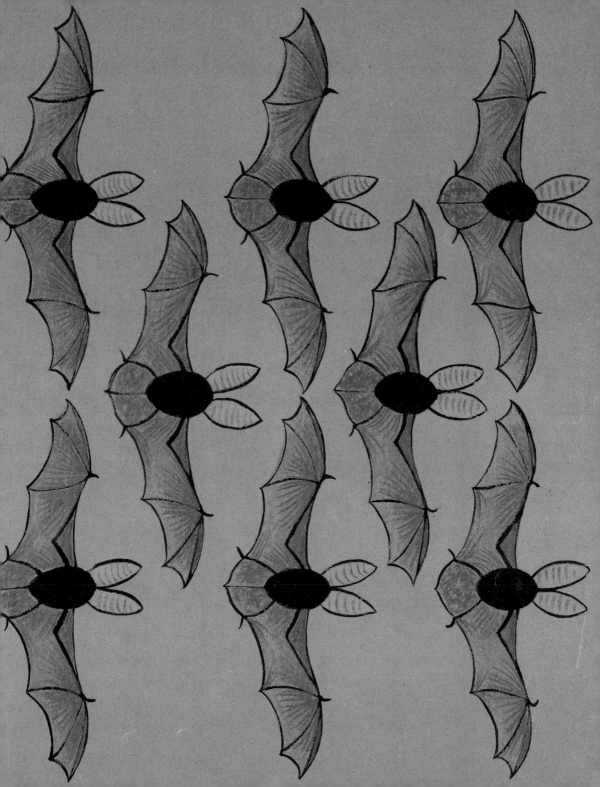

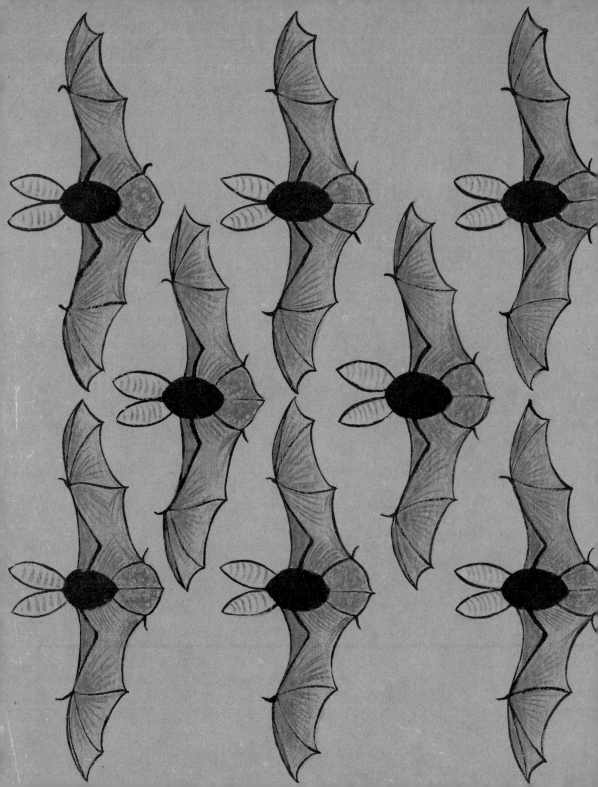